THE
REAL STORY
of
CHRISTMAS

THE
REAL STORY
of
CHRISTMAS

W. CLEON SKOUSEN

IZZARD INK
— PUBLISHING —

THE REAL STORY OF CHRISTMAS
BY W. CLEON SKOUSEN

© Copyright 1949, 1951, 1966, 1986, and 2018

Print Edition ISBN: 9781630729134
eBook ISBN: 9781630729127

Find The Real Story of Christmas at:
http://izzardink.com/product/real-story-christmas
http://www.therealstoryofchristmas.com

Interior Design by Alissa Rose Theodor

Published by Izzard Ink, LLC
Izzard Ink Publishing
PO BOX 522251
Salt Lake City, UT 84152
https://izzardink.com/
info@izzardink.com

CONTENTS

FOREWORD

THE STORY BEHIND THE REAL STORY OF CHRISTMAS

An amazing fulfillment of prophecy unfolded in 1948 just as W. Cleon Skousen was finishing the research and writing for *The Real Story of Christmas*.

It was May 14 when a little-noticed announcement slipped into a few radio broadcasts that day. It originated from a hot, scrubby corner of the desert on the east coast of the Mediterranean, a speck of land that had been in bloody dispute for centuries.

That afternoon local time, a man named David Ben-Gurion stood in the Tel Aviv Art Museum and declared: "We hereby proclaim the establishment of the Jewish state in Palestine, to be called Israel." And with that, the State of Israel became a sovereign nation.

For Skousen it was the thrilling fulfillment of ancient prophecy that he had written about just ten years earlier in his book, *Prophecy and Modern Times*.

Summarizing the words of Isaiah, Ezekiel, Jeremiah, Zechariah, Amos, Moses, and others, Skousen wrote about the rise of the Jewish nation:

"The Jewish prophets rejoiced in the coming of this, our day, although, as we shall see, they foresaw it to be an unprecedented era of persecution and suffering for their people. They rejoiced, however, as they saw the raising up of the Jewish Zion and the long await-ed arrival of their King Emmanuel. Eventually, they knew their King would come in majesty and power, delivering the besieged city of Jerusalem and reigning over his chosen people in supreme splendor that would attract the fealty [humble loyalty] of every nation un-der heaven."

The establishment of Israel also meant the reclaiming of the most sacred city on earth: the City of David called Jerusalem. This historic site is a revered place for half the world's population—for more than 2 billion Christians, 1-1/2 billion Muslims, and millions of Jews.

Palestine is the setting for *The Real Story of Christmas.* Today it is a liberated land where visitors may come to visit, to tour, and to worship free and unmolested, re-gardless of their nationality, race, or religion.

Traveling to a free Palestine impacted Skousen's sub-sequent revisions of *The Real Story of Christmas.* Begin-ning in the 1960s, Skousen led tours to Israel two and three times a year. This exposure helped him better cap-ture the setting and arrangement of events leading up to the birth of Jesus Christ.

The Real Story of Christmas was popular with Chris-tian audiences in many parts of the United States. Thou-sands of copies sold each year around Christmas time, and has to date sold more than 500,000 copies in print and recording. In 1969, *The Real Story of Christmas* was in its tenth printing when the Deseret Book Company decided to dramatize it with music. They chose famed actor and voice artist, Francis Urry, to do the narration. The production was broadcast during the Christmas season on KSL radio for decades afterward.

Skousen said he wrote the book to strip away the distractions surrounding the birth of Jesus so that its simple and beautiful story could stand on its own. By providing historical context and a clear explanation of the events, the people, and the places involved, the reader is quickly transported to a pivotal time in human history when the Romans ruled the world. In those days there was no hope of escape for the beleaguered Jews—at least not until one evening in early spring when there was born a babe in a manger who would change everything.

Skousen spent much of his adult life writing and warning about the darkness of Roman-type tyranny and oppression that today is a harsh reality for many hundreds of millions in the earth. But it won't stay that way, he said. The same prophets who foresaw the Jews returning to their homelands also foretold of another event that was coming. It would be the coming of the Messiah, the king of kings, the Lord of lords, who will reign forever and ever, and bring to the peoples of the earth, in Skousen's words, "... a glorious day, perhaps much nearer than we think, a day that men will call the Millennium—a Christmas season of peace on earth that will last a thousand years."

The birth of that glorious promise begins in a humble little village, long besieged by warriors, as described in the pages that follow. It is *The Real Story of Christmas.*

Paul B. Skousen
DECEMBER 25, 2017

THE REAL STORY OF CHRISTMAS

THERE NEVER WAS a more exciting Christmas than the first one. Oddly enough, however, the complete, historical account of that first Christmas is seldom told. There are forgotten chapters buried in scriptural records which the pageants at Christmas time fail to relate. The purpose of this writing is to try and tell the whole story the way history has preserved it.

THE HISTORICAL SETTING

PERHAPS WE SHOULD first remind ourselves that Jesus was born in a conquered country. More than sixty years before his birth the iron-shod wheels of Roman chariots had thundered through the streets of Jerusalem, and Pompey had planted the Roman eagles on Mount Zion.

Other Roman conquerors had followed, but in the end Augustus Caesar placed in power a cruel and cunning Arab to rule the Jewish people. His name was Herod — Herod the Great.

Herod pretended to be a convert to the Jewish faith. He began the construction of a magnificent temple. He even married a Jewish princess named Mariamne.[1] She bore him two sons, but they never lived to become rulers in Judea. Herod, their father, had committed murder to secure his throne, and when he saw the people wildly acclaiming Mariamne and her two half-Jewish sons, he ordered the three of them assassinated.[2] For this and Herod's other crimes the people deeply despised him.[3]

THE STORY OF CHRISTMAS
BEGINS IN THE TEMPLE

I N THE YEAR of the Romans, 752,[4] when Herod was past sixty, the central portion of the new temple was practically completed. It was here that the real story of Christmas begins.

On a certain day an ancient Levite priest came to the temple to preside at the altar. His name was Zacharias.[5] While the congregation waited without, Zacharias entered the room where the altar stood. It was called the Holy Place. As Zacharias stood there alone he saw straight before him the sacred veil behind which lay the Holy of Holies. In front of the veil was the golden altar with its dying embers from the incense-

1 Josephus, War of the Jews, Book 1:3.
2 Frederic W. Farrar, The Life of Christ, p. 51.
3 Josephus, War of the Jews, Book 14, Chapter 9:4.
4 James E. Talmage, Jesus the Christ. The year cited in this source is 753 for the birth of the Savior. Since the Christmas story begins one year earlier, the Roman date of 752 is used.
5 Luke 1:5.

burning of the night before. To his right Zacharias saw the table of shewbread and to his left stood the golden candlestick which furnished the only light.[6]

Zacharias had come to the temple this day with a prayer which had been the burden of his soul for many years. He longed for a son. Although the time had long since passed when he could expect a son, nevertheless, by habit, he continued to present his supplication to the Lord. It was the thought uppermost in his mind as he approached the altar of incense.

Suddenly Zacharias stopped. He was almost blinded as the dim half-light of the Holy Place was shattered by the brilliant appearance of a glorious being. An angel stood to the right of the altar surrounded by an intense, heavenly light.[7] For the first time in more than 400 years of Hebrew history, a revelation had been granted to a priest of the Jewish people.

FIRST APPEARANCE OF THE CHRISTMAS MESSENGER

IN TERROR ZACHARIAS began to retreat, but the holy messenger spoke to him, "Fear not, Zacharias," he said, "for thy prayer is heard and thy wife, Elisabeth, shall bear thee a son, and thou shalt call his name John." The humble Levite priest could scarcely believe his ears. The angel continued: "He shall be great in the sight

---

6 Luke 1:11.
7 J. Reuben Clark, Wist Ye Not That I Must Be About My Father's Business? p. 70. See cut and explanatory note

of the Lord ... and shall make ready a people prepared for the Lord."[8]

This was too much for Zacharias. How could Elisabeth have a son? It was impossible! She was too old. In this doubting spirit he challenged the angel.

"Whereby shall I know this? I am an old man and my wife is well-stricken in years."[9]

The eyes that looked down on Zacharias must have been deep as eternity. Did Zacharias doubt the power of God? Had he forgotten the mother of Samson, the mother of Samuel and the mother of Isaac -- all of whom received their children through a special blessing from heaven? Or did he doubt the authority of the angel?

In tones of solemn rebuke the angel declared: "I am Gabriel that stands in the presence of God; and I am sent to speak unto thee, and to show thee these glad tidings. Behold, thou shalt be dumb and not able to speak because thou believest not my words!"[10]

Instantly the angel was gone.

Almost as though he were stunned, Zacharias turned to fulfill the rite of burning of incense. As the clouds of perfumed vapor ascended above the partition, the Levite priest walked out before the people.

Why had he been so long? Zacharias tried to explain but his tongue was speechless. Finally, with si-

8 Luke 1:13-14.
9 Luke 1:18.
10 Luke 1:20.

lent gestures he made them understand he had seen a vision.[11]

NAZARETH—THE RESIDENCE
OF FORGOTTEN ROYALTY

ONE HUNDRED MILES north of Jerusalem lay a certain shallow valley sheltered by the hills of Galilee. In the days of which we speak there nestled in this valley a modest peasant village called Nazareth. Here lived a certain daughter of Israel who was to become one of the most famous women in the world. Her name was Miryam. Today we call her "Mary," but this is merely the modern translation of her name as it has come down to us through the Greek.

Miryam was a very popular name among the Jews.[12] Perhaps this was because their prophets had predicted, as had the prophets of the Nephites, that this would be the name of the Messiah's mother.[13]

By right of birth Miriam was a Jewish princess. She was a direct descendant of King David. In fact, only recently she had become betrothed to a young man who was also of the royal Davidic line. His name was Joseph. But at this particular time the fact that two young heirs to the throne of David were living in the obscure village of Nazareth was of little consequence, Poverty and the mad political scramble of ruthless world conquerors had

11 Luke 1:22.
12 Encyclopedia Americana, 1946 Edition, Vol. 18, p. 345, under "Mary."
13 Mosiah 3:8.

left the natural heirs to the throne of David forgotten and unnamed.

SECOND APPEARANCE OF THE CHRISTMAS MESSENGER

I T WAS PROBABLY in the month of August, and just six months after Gabriel appeared to Zacharias, that he also appeared to Mary in Nazareth.[14]

She was alone when the celestial vision opened before her. As with Zacharias, she was deeply frightened. The sudden brilliance of the heavenly messenger momentarily overwhelmed her and even before she could speak, the salutation of the glorious Gabriel fell upon her ears. "Hail, thou that are highly favoured. The Lord is with thee! Blessed art thou among women!"

Instinctively Mary drew back, but with comforting assurance the angel quickly added, "Fear not, Mary, for thou hast found favour with God."

Then in solemn words designed to inspire confidence and understanding he delivered his precious message: "Behold, thou shalt conceive and bring forth a son. He shall be called Jesus, the Son of the Highest, and the Lord God shall give unto him the throne of his father, David."

Mary could not comprehend. "How shall this be?" she asked.

14 Luke 1:26.

"The Holy Ghost shall come upon thee, and the power of the Highest shall overshadow thee. Therefore that which shall be born of thee shall be called the Son of God."

Mary responded to this thrilling message with words which reflect the depth of her spirituality and the beauty of her character.

"Behold the handmaid of the Lord," she said. "Be it unto me according to thy word."

WHO WAS GABRIEL?

IT IS DOUBTFUL that either Mary or Zacharias knew the true identity of this angel who called himself Gabriel.

Nevertheless, this heavenly harbinger must have thrilled as he stood before this beautiful girl. He knew she was a person of nobility. He knew that her identity and mission had been revealed to the prophet's centuries before she was born.[15] Gabriel also knew that Mary was one of his own descendants.

This messenger from heaven who called himself Gabriel was none other than the prophet Noah.[16] As Mary looked up into his brilliant countenance she was beholding the un-resurrected spirit of her own great patriarchal ancestor.

When he had finished delivering his message Gabriel confided to Mary that her aged cousin, Elisabeth,

---

15 1 Nephi 11:18; Mosiah 5:8; Alma 7:10.
16 History of the Church 3:386.

had also conceived and that already she was in her sixth month.[17] Then he departed.

Left to herself, Mary treasured up the words of the angel in secret. Neither her parents nor even Joseph

---

17 Luke 1:36.

whom she deeply loved were informed. Nevertheless, there was one person with whom she felt she might share her sacred knowledge. That was Elisabeth. Therefore, she made haste to go straightway and visit her.

Sometime prior to Mary's departure, however -- perhaps it was only a few days before -- the glory of God encompassed her and for Mary the miracle of new life began.[18]

THE MOTHER OF JESUS VISITS THE MOTHER OF JOHN THE BAPTIST

Z ACHARIAS AND ELISABETH lived in the hill country of Judea not far from Jerusalem. It was a difficult journey of a hundred miles over treacherous roads. When Mary arrived at her cousin's home Elisabeth rose to greet her. The older woman stretched out her hands to the young girl and being moved by the Spirit of the Lord she exclaimed fervently: "Blessed are thou among women, and blessed is the fruit of thy womb." Then she added humbly, "And whence is this ... that the mother of my Lord should come unto me?"

Realizing that Elisabeth already knew her great secret, Mary replied simply, "My soul doth magnify the Lord."[19]

During the following three months Mary stayed with Elisabeth to await the time when Elisabeth would be

18 See James E. Talmage, Jesus the Christ, pp. 83-84.
19 Luke 1:46.

delivered of her child. And when her baby came it was a male child just as Gabriel had predicted.

For Zacharias and Elisabeth this baby was a triumphant blessing. Relatives, neighbors and friends joined in their rejoicing and all of them gathered to witness the naming of this wonderful infant born out of season.

JOHN THE BAPTIST IS NAMED AND ORDAINED

NOT UNTIL THE ceremony was actually in progress, however, did the officiating priest determine the baby's name. Then he found himself in the midst of a family dispute. Elisabeth said the name of the child should be John. Indignant male relatives ordered the priest to name him after his father.

Finally, when Elisabeth continued to object, an appeal was made to Zacharias. This was done by signs, for he was deaf as well as without speech.[20] Zacharias motioned for a tablet, and when they obtained one he wrote with the stencil, "His name is John." This caused all the relatives to marvel. They thought surely the devout Levite would want his only child to bear the name of its father.

But in a moment they had more cause for astonishment. Zacharias suddenly began to speak. For the first time in nearly a year, his tongue was loosed. "Blessed be the Lord God of Israel" he exclaimed. Then gazing

20 Luke 1:62.

proudly on his infant son and being filled with the spirit of prophecy, Zacharias declared: "Thou, child, shalt be called the prophet of the Highest; for thou shalt go before the face of the Lord to prepare his ways."[21]

Later that same day, probably in the privacy of their own home, an angel came and ordained the infant John to the Priesthood.[22] Never before in history had such a procedure been followed, but here was a choice child, filled with the Holy Ghost from the time of his birth. Of him the Savior himself would later say: "Among those that are born of women there is not a greater prophet than John the Baptist."[23]

MARY RETURNS TO NAZARETH

Now mary returned to her home in Nazareth and there Joseph anxiously awaited her.

How long it was before he learned she was with child we do not know, but when he did become aware of it he was overwhelmed with grief. Under the Jewish law a betrothal was almost as binding as marriage itself and faithlessness was punishable by death.[24] The only alternative was to "put her away" by a bill of public divorcement.[25] Joseph was not bitter against Mary, only sorrowful, and therefore he resolved to "put her away privily."[26]

21 Luke 1:76.
22 D&C 84:28.
23 Luke 7:28.
24 Deuteronomy 22:23.
25 Deuteronomy 24:1.
26 Matthew 1:19.

During this moment of deep emotional strain, no word of explanation escaped Mary's lips. In fact, she herself was probably without knowledge concerning the will of the Lord on this subject. She knew not but what her sacred mission might require her to forfeit her betrothal to Joseph.

In the dark hours of the night, while Joseph feverishly pondered the sudden shipwreck of his prospective marriage, the angel of the Lord appeared in a dream and said: "Joseph, thou son of David, fear not to take unto thee Mary thy wife; for that which is conceived in her is of the Holy Ghost. She shall bring forth a son, and thou shalt call his name Jesus: for he shall save his people from their sins."[27]

Who will describe the transitional joy which flooded the mind of Joseph as this revelation brought to him a beautiful and sympathetic understanding of Mary's sacred calling? And who will record the tender scene when he confided to Mary that now he shared her secret?

Joseph's marriage to Mary must have followed immediately, for the angel commanded it, and by the time of the taxing or census ordered by Caesar, Joseph and Mary are specifically referred to as husband and wife.[28]

WHEN WAS JESUS BORN?

I T WAS EARLY in April, in the year of the Romans, 753, that Joseph and Mary came to Bethlehem.

27 Matthew 1:20-21.
28 Luke 9:5.

The exact date of these events was not certainly known until 1830 when the Lord affirmed that April 6th of that year marked one thousand eight hundred and thirty years since the Savior was born in the flesh.[29] Prior to that time no one knew the precise date. Authorities conceded, however, that December 25th was not celebrated as Christmas until the fourth century A.D. And it was established on that date simply for convenience. December 25th was chosen because at that time it was celebrated as a national holiday honoring the birth of the Roman god, Sol.[30] It was fitting that the true date of the Savior's nativity should be affirmed through divine revelation.

Since Bethlehem was originally the "City of David" it was therefore the ancestral home of both Mary and Joseph. In other parts of the world the Roman government had required each person to register for the taxation at his place of residence. In Palestine, however, the Jews were allowed to follow their ancient custom of returning to the region of their forefathers to be registered. For this reason Mary and Joseph had come to Bethlehem.

Being of modest circumstances and because Mary's delicate condition required that they travel slowly, Joseph and Mary did not arrive in the vicinity of Bethlehem until long after that notable city had begun to overflow with large crowds from much less distant regions. Jerusalem itself was only six miles away, and unaccommodated crowds from the national capital added to the

29 D&C 20:1.
30 Encyclopedia Americana, 1946 Edition, Vol. 6, p. 623, under "Christmas."

congestion at Bethlehem. In fact, this was also the season for the feast of the Passover. This alone would bring tens of thousands to Jerusalem and nearby communities like Bethlehem.

THE FIRST CHRISTMAS EVE

As JOSEPH AND Mary neared the end of this long journey they passed flocks of sheep grazing upon the hills. Here their great ancestor, David, had tended flocks in his youth. Here Ruth, their maternal ancestor, had gleaned the fields of grain.

To Mary and Joseph this was home and every foot of it seemed saturated with sacred history.

But the City of David did not welcome them. As they threaded their way among the teeming crowds of Bethlehem, Joseph must have felt increasing apprehension. Where would they stay? Everywhere they met with the same rebuff: "No room!"

As time passed the situation became desperate. Knowing Mary's great mission it must have seemed incomprehensible to Joseph that all doors should close against them. Could not there be some help? Surely there must be some place of comfort and convenience for a young mother already feeling the imminent travail of childbirth. But to all his pleas he was turned away. "No room!"

Overwhelmed with anxiety, Joseph was finally forced to accept what he normally would have rejected with disgust. A stable. His soul must have been harrowed to the quick as he led his trembling young wife into this humble abode made for cattle. In haste he prepared for her the most meager semblance of comfort. No doubt he secured what help he could from the nearby inn, but at best it would have been grossly inadequate. No other king was ever born into the world under so humble a circumstance.

In the year of the Romans, 753, the Jewish nation never dreamed that this was the year of their salvation; the time when their long-awaited Messiah would be born. In the celestial courts of heavenly places the seraphic hosts of angels stood at solemn attention waiting for the Great Jehovah to take the step which would usher him into the forgetfulness of the Second Estate. This was the moment which would divide history. No doubt the ancient saints from Adam to Malachi waited tensely as they saw the great drama about to begin.

Only a mile distant, hovering near the outskirts of the city, certain angels prepared to make their presence known. Shepherds, abiding in the fields and watching their flocks by night, were chosen to be the recipients of a magnificent vision. It commenced the very moment Mary's precious infant was born. Immediately the shepherds saw the veil of mortality sheared back, and an angel stood before them with a glory which enveloped the scene in a radiant light.

The shepherds thought they would be consumed and shrank back in fear, but the angel said: "Fear not; for behold, I bring you good tidings of great joy, which shall be to all people. For unto you is born this day in the city of David a Saviour, which is Christ the Lord. And this shall be a sign unto you, ye shall find the babe wrapped in swaddling clothes, lying in a manger."[31]

At such a moment the hosts of heaven could be held back no longer. The majestic choir of former-day saints burst into song. The shepherds heard them sing: "Glory to God in the highest, and on earth peace, good will toward men."[32]

When the vision closed, the shepherds left immediately to go into the town and seek out the location of "the child lying in a manger." Perhaps the flickering flame of a tallow lamp sent its rays into the night to guide them to the stable's portals. And when they had gathered round they found the babe truly wrapped in swaddling clothes and cradled in a manger.

But in addition to that there was nothing unusual in the nativity scene to impress them with its power. They simply beheld a humble Galilean peasant and his wife with a newborn child. There were no halos of light about their persons, no visible cherubim. Nevertheless, with the glory of the angels still fresh in their minds, the shepherds looked upon the sleeping child with devotion and awe. Jehovah had entered mortality!

31 Luke 2:10-12.
32 Luke 2:14.

THE UNKNOWN KING

WHEN THE SHEPHERDS finally left the stable they ran swiftly to awaken their friends and neighbors. To all who would listen they related the wonderful night vision and the things they had been told concerning this newborn child. But the people were not impressed. The scripture says they merely "wondered."[33] Nevertheless, this did not dampen the ardor of the shepherds. They returned to their flocks "glorifying and praising God for all the things they had heard and seen."[34]

And so the early morning hours of the first Christmas passed without further incident. While the baby slept, Mary treasured in her heart the thrilling triumph of this hour.

And where were the Wise Men? Although Christmas pageants have it otherwise there were no Wise Men present on the night of nativity. In fact, their homeland was far away to "the East." During the early hours of this first Christmas morning they, like the Nephites, were in their own country rejoicing at the sudden appearance of a great new star in the heavens.[35] The prophets had said this star was the sign by which they would know that the Savior had been born.[36] Therefore, the Wise Men promptly prepared to depart for the land of Palestine. They wanted to see this wonderful child and give him

33 Luke 2:18.
34 Luke 2:20.
35 3 Nephi 1:21; Matthew 2:2.
36 Helaman 14:5.

their gifts of devotion. But it was a long journey. As we shall see in a moment, the scripture is plain that it was weeks or perhaps even months before the Wise Men arrived in Bethlehem.

Meanwhile Mary and Joseph prepared to fulfill the laws and ordinances prescribed for a newborn child. When the baby was eight days old he was taken to the priest for naming. The name which they gave him was "Joshua." This was a common name among the Jews, but it was the name the angel had designated. In later life the people called him "Joshua of Nazareth" to distinguish him from all other men bearing the same name. Today we call him "Jesus." But "Jesus" is simply the modified Greek equivalent for the name of Joshua. This name symbolizes the mission of the Savior, for it means, "Jehovah is our Salvation."[37]

JESUS IS PRESENTED IN THE TEMPLE

FOLLOWING THIS MARY waited and rested for thirty-two days until the prescribed period of "purification" was accomplished. Then Joseph and Mary made the six-mile journey into Jerusalem to present Jesus in the temple. Dedicating this first-born son to the service of God was one of the requirements of the Law of Moses.[38]

It was also required that Mary offer a young lamb and a dove as a sacrifice. However, in the case of poor people,

37 Frederic W. Farrar, The Life of Christ, p. 35 and note.
38 Exodus 13:2.

two doves were acceptable. It is significant that Mary's offering was two doves.[39]

Living in Jerusalem at this time was a wise and devout Jew named Simeon. So faithful had he been that the Lord had blessed him with a direct revelation promising him that he should not die until he had seen the Great Messiah.

On this day as he pursued his business in the city, the Holy Ghost suddenly came upon him. It bade him hasten to the temple. Simeon arrived just as the ceremony was beginning. Being constrained of the Spirit, he hastened forward and tenderly took the young child from his mother and held him in his arms. With deepest emotion Simeon raised his face up toward heaven and said: "O Lord, now lettest thou thy servant depart in peace; for mine eyes have seen thy salvation.... A light to lighten the Gentiles and the glory of thy people Israel!"[40]

Then Simeon turned to Mary and in the spirit of prophecy told her of the greatness of the mission her child would perform. He also warned her of the suffering which she, as his mother, would be required to bear -- a suffering that would be like the piercing of her soul by a sword.[41] Thirty-three years later at the foot of the Cross on Calvary, Mary learned the literal significance of Simeon's tragic prophecy.

There was also in the temple at this time a very devout and famous woman who enjoyed the spirit of prophecy.

39 Luke 2:24.
40 Luke 2:25-32.
41 Luke 2:35.

She was a widow, eighty-four years of age, who served in the temple night and day. Her name was Anna and she likewise received a testimony of the Holy Ghost that Jesus was the long-awaited Messiah. She bore testimony to those who were present and gave thanks unto God that she had lived to see the Savior.[42]

Following the ceremony, Joseph and Mary returned with Jesus to Bethlehem. By this time they had obtained residence in "a house" which Matthew specifically mentions.[43]

THE COMING OF THE WISE MEN

Now it was sometime after this that wise men came to Jerusalem seeking the newborn King of the Jews. Being without guile and innocent of the state of affairs in this part of the world, they went naively to Herod, thinking he would be informed of the identity and whereabouts of the new king. But Herod was greatly disturbed by their words. Such convictions as these men carried would surely give credence to certain stories which were rapidly spreading among the common people -- stories which had originated with certain shepherds who solemnly testified that the Christ-child indeed had been born.[44]

Hurriedly, Herod conferred with the priests and learned scribes. Where did tradition and prophecy say their king would be born? "In Bethlehem, the City of

42 Luke 2:36-38.
43 Matthew 2:11; Frederic W. Farrar, The Life of Christ, p. 31.
44 Luke 2:17.

David," they said.[45] Frantically, Herod conjured up a scheme. Surely he must not stand by after all he had done -- even to the killing of his own wife and children -- and allow his throne to be snatched away by some nefarious pretender whom the Superstitious populace might raise up to claim as their long-awaited Messiah or divine King! In this spirit of desperate hatred he plotted murder for the child, whoever he was.

Calling the wise men to him "privily," he extracted from them the precise date when the great new star had first been seen in their own country.[46] When they had told him, Herod made them promise to try and find the child and then inform him so that he might come and worship the new king also. The wise men consented and departed.

Speedily and at night they made their way to Bethlehem. En route they rejoiced to behold once again the same brilliant star which they had previously seen in their own country marking the date of the Savior's birth. They seemed to be led to the place where he was, but it did not turn out to be a stable. Joseph and Mary had long since found better accommodations. Matthew says the Wise Men went into "the house" and there they knelt before the child and worshipped him.[47] Then they opened their treasures and presented him with gifts of gold, frankincense and myrrh.

Later when the time came for the Wise Men to depart, the angel of the Lord appeared to them in a dream and

45 Matthew 2:5-6.
46 Matthew 2:7.
47 Matthew 2:11.

told them not to go back to Herod but to return to "the East" by a separate way. This they did. Out of the unknown they came, into the unknown they departed. We know nothing more about them, neither their names, their number nor their nationality.[48] All else that has been said about them is fiction. Their only mark left on the pages of history comprises less than a dozen verses of scripture.

MASSACRE OF THE INNOCENTS

Meanwhile, herod impatiently awaited the return of the magi, but when all hope was exhausted he lashed out commands to his servile mercenaries to sweep down on Bethlehem and massacre every child under two years of age. Since Herod had specifically asked the Wise Men when the star first appeared which signified the Savior's birth, it is significant that he ordered all children to be slain who were under two years of age.

As the soldiers hastened to obey, they violently perpetrated one of the most horrible crimes ever inflicted upon a helpless community. But Jesus was not there. Scarcely had the wise men departed for the East before an angel warned Joseph to take Mary and Jesus into Egypt.[49] There they waited safely while the lethal hatred of Herod robbed the weeping mothers in Bethlehem of all their youngest children.

48 James E. Talmage, Jesus the Christ, p. 99.
49 Matthew 2:13.

But even as Herod ordered this terrible "slaughter of the innocents," the grim reaper of retribution reached out to snatch his own life away.

At the very moment when he would have sold his soul to keep his throne, Herod found himself dying of a most loathsome disease.[50]

His last few days were spent in the greatest agony. Five days before the end he tried to commit suicide. With death hovering near, Herod found his closest courtiers rebelling against him. Before his very eyes, the kingdom began crumbling away.[51] In less than a hundred years the last descendant of this infamous character would be erased from the face of the earth.

Death was finally a welcome release to Herod's fevered and tortured body. For the people, his passing was a blessing. They celebrated with a joyous festival.[52]

Down along the banks of the tropical Nile, Joseph and Mary waited with the infant Jesus. Then, even before messengers could bring word to the general populace, Joseph was told by the angel that Herod was dead. Immediately they prepared to return to their homeland.

Apparently Joseph and Mary had hoped to live permanently in Bethlehem, but as their little caravan neared the region they learned that Herod's cruel son, Archelaus, ruled this part of the kingdom. Tired as they were, they continued their journey and passed on up into the

---

50 Frederic W. Farrar, The Life of Christ, p. 54.
51 Frederic W. Farrar, The Life of Christ, p. 54.
52 Frederic W. Farrar, The Life of Christ, p. 55.

hills of Galilee, finally arriving in Nazareth. There they resolved to make their home.

In all these circumstances three great prophecies were literally fulfilled: that Jesus would be born in Bethlehem,[53] that he would come up out of Egypt,[54] and finally, that he would be called a native of Nazareth.[55]

Though each prophecy seemed to contradict the other two, nevertheless, in the wisdom of heaven, all three found complete fulfillment. In the life of the Savior, no promise of any prophet concerning him was left un-reconciled.

As the years passed by the scripture says, "Jesus increased in wisdom and stature and in favour with God and man." Gradually he learned his true identity. He was taught by ministering angels. At the age of thirty-three he was finally prepared to ascend the heights of the mortal mission to which he was born. At the last moment he could have turned back. But he did not. He passed beneath all things that he might save all things -- the human race, the earth and all the life that ever embellished it. The purpose of the Savior's mission was broader than many have supposed.

THE REAL SPIRIT OF CHRISTMAS

HERE, THEN, WE conclude the known history of Christmas. All else that is added is man's homemade invention —

53 Micah 5:2.
54 Hosea 11:1.
55 Matthew 2:23.

the pleasant, lighted tree comes down to us from the days of heathen Rome, the holly wreaths and mistletoe from the ancient, mystic Druids, the exciting visit of St. Nicholas from fourth century Christian tradition and the happy, jolly Santa Claus from pure modern imagination.[56]

But with it all, the most important thing still survives — the spirit of peace on earth, good will toward men.

Never at any other season does peace come closer to a universal reality than at Christmas time. More friends are remembered and more enemies forgiven than at any other time of the year. It is but a shadow of things to come.

Not far from us and surrounded by his legions of heavenly hosts, this same Jesus works today toward the time when he will come back to the earth. It will be a glorious day; perhaps much nearer than we think, and when it arrives, men will call it the Millennium — a Christmas season of peace on earth that will last a thousand years.

56 Encyclopedia Americana, 1946 Edition, Vol. 6, p. 623, under "Christmas."

LUKE CHAPTER TWO
THE CHRISTMAS STORY

1. And it came to pass in those days, that there went out a decree from Cæsar Augustus, that all the world should be taxed.

2. (And this taxing was first made when Cyrenius was governor of Syria.)

3. And all went to be taxed, every one into his own city.

4. And Joseph also went up from Galilee, out of the city of Nazareth, into Judæa, unto the city of David, which is called Bethlehem; (because he was of the house and lineage of David:)

5. To be taxed with Mary his espoused wife, being great with child.

6. And so it was, that, while they were there, the days were accomplished that she should be delivered.

7. And she brought forth her firstborn son, and wrapped him in swaddling clothes, and laid him in a manger; because there was no room for them in the inn.

8. And there were in the same country shepherds abiding in the field, keeping watch over their flock by night.

9. And, lo, the angel of the Lord came upon them, and the glory of the Lord shone round about them: and they were sore afraid.

10. And the angel said unto them, Fear not: for, behold, I bring you good tidings of great joy, which shall be to all people.

11. For unto you is born this day in the city of David a Saviour, which is Christ the Lord.

12. And this shall be a sign unto you; Ye shall find the babe wrapped in swaddling clothes, lying in a manger.

13. And suddenly there was with the angel a multitude of the heavenly host praising God, and saying,

14. Glory to God in the highest, and on earth peace, good will toward men.

15. And it came to pass, as the angels were gone away from them into heaven, the shepherds said one to another, Let us now go even unto Bethlehem, and see this thing which is come to pass, which the Lord hath made known unto us.

16. And they came with haste, and found Mary, and Joseph, and the babe lying in a manger.

17. And when they had seen it, they made known abroad the saying which was told them concerning this child.

18. And all they that heard it wondered at those things which were told them by the shepherds.

19. But Mary kept all these things, and pondered them in her heart.

20. And the shepherds returned, glorifying and praising God for all the things that they had heard and seen, as it was told unto them.